The Sleepy Way to Survive

by Tom Poulson

Harcourt

SCHOOL PUBLISHERS

Cover, ©MARK RAYCROFT/Minden Pictures; p.3, ©Charles George/Visuals Unlimited; p.4, ©PhotoDisc; p.5, p.8, p.14, ©Corel; p.6, p.9, ©Tom McHugh/Photo Researchers, Inc.; p.7, ©Corbis; p.10, ©Gustav Verderber/Visuals Unlimited; p.11, ©John M. Burnley/Photo Researchers, Inc.; p.12, ©George McCarthy/CORBIS; p.13, ©Millard H. Sharp/Photo Researchers, Inc.

Printed in China

ISBN 10: 0-15-351526-0
ISBN 13: 978-0-15-351526-2

Ordering Options
ISBN 10: 0-15-351214-8 (Grade 4 Advanced Collection)
ISBN 13: 978-0-15-351214-8 (Grade 4 Advanced Collection)
ISBN 10: 0-15-358116-6 (package of 5)
ISBN 13: 978-0-15-358116-8 (package of 5)

5 6 7 8 9 10 985 12 11 10 09

It's the middle of January, and the temperature in northern Alaska is –25° Fahrenheit (–31°C). The frozen ground is covered by snow. Strong winds blow, making the air even colder. At night, the temperature drops even more.

A casual observer might be lured into thinking that there's not a single creature alive in this harsh environment. That observation would be incorrect, for under the ground, in a small burrow, lies an Arctic ground squirrel.

The Arctic ground squirrel resembles the gray squirrels that are common in the United States. On this day, this squirrel in the Arctic is not climbing a tree or running through someone's yard like a gray squirrel. Instead, it is curled up in a ball and lying still. Its body temperature is almost as cold as the temperature outside, and it takes only two or three breaths each minute. The squirrel is not ill or dying. Instead, it is in a state of dormancy.

Some animals have the ability to become dormant. The word *dormant* means "temporarily inactive or not in use." An animal ready to become dormant will usually go to a safe place. It will then enter a sleep-like state. Nearly all of the animal's normal body functions slow down or stop. For example, its body temperature may drop. It may breathe less. Its heartbeat may be lower. Some animals, while dormant, are very close to being dead.

Dormancy is a very helpful trait. It helps animals survive. Most animals that become dormant do so because their environment has changed in some way. For example, it may get very cold or hot. The water may dry up. Maybe there is little food. Animals become dormant in order to protect themselves. By avoiding these conditions, animals have a greater chance of survival.

Animals that become dormant have another advantage. Dormancy allows them to live in habitats where many other animals *cannot* live. For example, some animals cannot live in hot deserts. Others cannot live in regions where it gets very cold. There are fewer animals living in these environments. When many animals live in one place, they have to compete with one another for the available food. When there are fewer animals, there is less competition. There is more food to go around.

Typical gray squirrels could not survive in the harsh environment of the Arctic. The Arctic ground squirrel *can* live there because it can become dormant. This means that the Arctic ground squirrel does not need to compete with other animals for food during the long winter.

The most common reason animals become dormant is the air temperature. Many desert animals become dormant during the hot days of summer. Many animals in cool regions, such as the Arctic, become dormant during the bitter cold winter months.

Another reason animals become dormant is the water supply. If the available water in an area dries up, some animals may enter a dormant state. The African lungfish lives in swamps and small rivers in western and southern Africa. If the water in the area dries up, the lungfish burrows into the mud. It curls up and becomes inactive. While dormant, the lungfish's gills stop working. It then mimics a mammal and breathes air through its mouth.

You have probably already learned that bears "hibernate" during the winter. Hibernation is one kind of dormancy. Animals become dormant in different ways based on their body temperatures. Some animals are cold-blooded, and some are warm-blooded.

The bodies of cold-blooded animals are the same temperature as the air. If the air becomes warm, the animal's body temperature goes up. If the air cools, the animal's body temperature goes down. Fish and reptiles are cold-blooded.

Warm-blooded animals, though, keep the same body temperature. Their temperature stays about the same whether it is cold or hot. Humans are warm-blooded. The temperature of the human body is always around 98.6° Fahrenheit (37°C). Bears, cats, and horses are some examples of warm-blooded animals.

When cold-blooded animals become dormant, their body temperature drops. These animals are not able to control their own body temperatures. The air temperature determines their body temperature. Also, these animals cannot decide on their own when they will stop being dormant as some other animals can. Instead, outside factors, such as the weather or the amount of water in the area, determine when they will "wake up."

Frogs and salamanders are cold-blooded. As winter approaches, they become dormant. Many frogs and salamanders climb into rotting logs near the waterways where they live. Some will burrow into the mud at the bottom of the waterway. Others will burrow into the bank of the waterway. Toads live on land. They usually lay dormant in burrows they make.

Reptiles are another kind of cold-blooded animal.
Many reptiles can become dormant. Snakes, turtles,
and lizards are all reptiles. In winter, these reptiles
find a place where the temperature does not drop below
freezing. Usually, they go underground. Few reptiles
live in the Arctic or in Antarctica. That's because the soil
underground is always frozen. Reptiles aren't able to dig
into the frozen soil to lay dormant.

Snakes do not dig holes because they don't have claws.
They have to find a cave or pit. Some places do not have
enough open pits or holes for all the snakes that live there,
so the snakes lie dormant in large groups. People have
found places where over one hundred lay dormant!

Some snakes also become dormant during the hot days
of summer. They find a shady place, such as under a rock,
to stay cool until the sun goes down. Many snakes that live
in deserts do this.

Many people make the mistake of saying that frogs or snakes "hibernate." It is more accurate to say that these animals *become dormant*. Only warm-blooded animals actually hibernate.

The word *hibernation* is used to describe a dormant, warm-blooded animal in the winter. However, some warm-blooded animals lie dormant in the summer. When a warm-blooded animal lies dormant in the summer, it is called *estivation*.

Warm-blooded animals can decide for themselves when to enter into hibernation. For example, if there is a shortage of food, a warm-blooded animal can go off and hibernate. These animals can also choose to "wake up" from hibernation. Cold-blooded animals cannot do any of these things.

It is deceptive—and incorrect—to say that bears hibernate. Only a few warm-blooded animals hibernate. These include hedgehogs, bats, and rodents, such as hamsters and squirrels. These animals are "true hibernators." Bears, however, are "shallow hibernators."

The body temperature of a true hibernator becomes very, very low. For example, the Arctic ground squirrel's body temperature is normally around 100° Fahrenheit (37.7°C). When hibernating, its temperature is about 32° Fahrenheit (0°C). That's right around the temperature at which water freezes!

Shallow hibernators include bears, raccoons, and chipmunks. A bear's normal body temperature is also about 100° Fahrenheit (37.7°C). When it hibernates, though, its temperature drops only a few degrees to about 93° Fahrenheit (33°C). Obviously, that's not even close to freezing.

11

Many things happen to the bodies of true hibernators. The animal's heartbeat slows down, and it takes very few breaths. The internal organs, such as the heart, almost completely stop working. The animal loses about half of its body weight. Often the animal's bones and teeth weaken. The animal is in a state very close to death. In fact, some hibernating animals actually do die during hibernation.

True hibernators do not stay "asleep" the whole winter. Some of them will move around a little bit. Others will actually leave their burrows to try to find some food. Animals that have food stored in their den will sometimes eat some of it.

Shallow hibernators do not go into deep "sleep." Instead, they stay in their dens or burrows feeling sleepy. It is more like a long winter's rest than a true hibernation. These animals are able to move around and do things. For example, female bears give birth to their cubs during the winter hibernation.

Even though it is not true hibernation, shallow hibernation is still helpful. It lets the animals save energy and survive the long winter. Also, since the animals are not in a state of deep sleep, they can wake up and protect themselves from predators. For example, a raccoon in shallow hibernation would be able to sense a wolf nearby. Also, shallow-hibernating animals can leave their burrows if they need to. The raccoon, for example, would notice if its burrow were flooding with water.

When it is time, animals come out of hibernation at different rates. Some take only an hour or so to "wake up." Others, such as the Arctic ground squirrel, take about three hours. The animal's body systems start to slowly turn back "on." The heart starts to beat faster. The body temperature starts to increase. The animal starts to take more breaths. Usually, after about twenty-four hours, the animal is back to normal. It will stay that way until the next time nature requires the animal to go into a special kind of sleep that helps it to survive.

Think Critically

1. What determines the body temperature of cold-blooded animals?

2. Why would it be difficult for reptiles to live in the Arctic?

3. How does dormancy help animals?

4. How are true hibernators different from shallow hibernators?

5. What did you find surprising in this book? Why?

 Science

Write a Paragraph Choose an animal from this book. Find out more about how it hibernates. Then write a short report that explains what the animal does before, during, and after hibernation.

School-Home Connection Discuss this book with a family member. Then have a discussion about other survival strategies that animals use, such as migration and camouflage.